THE WAR OF INDEPENDENCE

THE WAR OF INDEPENDENCE

SEAN McMAHON

MERCIER PRESS

MERCIER PRESS

Cork

www.mercierpress.ie

Originally published in 2000.

This revised edition © Mercier Press, 2019.

ISBN: 978 1 78117 718 1

A CIP record for this title is available from the British Library.

Printed and bound in the EU.

CONTENTS

THE LEAD-UP TO WAR

AT MEENBANAD, a plateau halfway between Kincasslagh and Dungloe in the Rosses of Donegal, stands a slab monument with the following inscription in Irish and English:

> To commemorate the first action in the War of Independence; when the Irish Volunteers rescued two comrades, James Ward & James Duffy, from British Troops at this place on the 4th day of January 1918.

'This place' was then the last railway halt (known officially as Kincasslagh Road) before the terminus of the Londonderry and Lough Swilly Railway at Burtonport, and the Volunteers were removed from the train that was to take them to imprisonment in Derry. The action, carried out by a party of local men that included Fergus Ward and the brothers Dom and John Bonner, ante-dated by a year and seventeen days the incident that is conventionally regarded as the beginning of the Anglo-Irish War.

It was the first of several indications that con-stitutional methods of achieving the aim of 'old Ireland free' had been thrust aside by the Irish Volunteers. Unlike the majority of later incidents, however, it was bloodless – in sharp contrast to the action at Soloheadbeg, County Tipperary, on 21 January 1919 that resulted in the shooting of two policemen who were supervising the trans-port of gelignite to a quarry. That raid, carried out by nine Volunteers including Dan Breen and Seán Treacy, illustrated the daring and ruthlessness of the Volunteers and marked out members of the Royal Irish Constabulary (RIC) as the most vul-nerable part of the 'enemy'.

Like the Meenbanad operation, the Solo-headbeg raid was carried out on local initiative, without sanction from either the Volunteers' central command or the politicians who were, on that same day, taking their seats in Dáil Éireann, the new Irish parliament.

Irish Volunteers (l. to r.) Seumas Robinson, Seán Treacy, Dan Breen and Michael Brennan c. 1919. (Mercier Archive)

The Irish Volunteers had been set up in 1913 by Irish nationalists in response to the setting up of the unionist Ulster Volunteer Force (UVF) in the north of the country. While the UVF opposed the introduction of Home Rule, which would have given the island limited self-governance, the Irish Volunteers supported this promised parliamentary reform. However, with the start of the First World War, the postponement of the implementation of Home Rule, and the split of the Irish Volunteers, the new goal of the remaining, much reduced Volunteers quickly became full independence for Ireland. When the Easter Rising of 1916 failed, it was realised by the surviving leaders of the Volunteers that new tactics would be needed.

The Irish Constabulary had been created as a paramilitary, well-armed force in 1836 ('royal' was added in 1867, as a reward for its success in

fighting the Fenian rebellion in that year), but by the later decades of the nineteenth century it had become essentially a civil constabulary. By 1919 it had many long-serving members and was not equipped to fight the guerrilla tactics that would be used by the Volunteers in this new

A senior RIC officer.
(Mercier Archive)

conflict. Its members were conscious, too, that, whatever the outcome of the protracted political process, their days as a force were numbered; uncertainty about the future did not help morale.

The other Irish police force, the Dublin Metropolitan Police (DMP), was formed in the same year as the RIC, but its members were unarmed and prided themselves on being taller and grander than the RIC men.

By the time the Truce came into effect on 11 July 1921, the numbers of those killed comprised 433 police (including DMP officers), and over 1,000 military, IRA and civilians. The latter category is necessarily blurred, since it included not only active

Members of the DMP. (Mercier Archive)

Volunteers and, to use the modern euphemism, 'collateral' casualties, but also at least a hundred people that the local IRA commanders designated, often unjustly, as 'spies'. The 'collaterals' included people caught in crossfire, those who had 'failed to halt when challenged' by military or police patrols and, in a few cases, women and children killed in raids.

The roots of the conflict in Ireland lay in the British government's attitude towards the idea of Irish self-government. The need for the preservation of the union had exercised the minds of most British (and all Conservative) statesmen since the time of Sir Robert Peel (1788–1850). (It was his name, first associated with the early constabulary, the Peace Preservation Force formed in 1814, that caused the RIC to be known universally as 'Peelers'.) Peel believed that despite Ireland being endlessly troublesome (except for the loyal counties of the north-east), this was a small price to pay for the maintenance of the integrity of the growing British Empire.

By the time of the death of Queen Victoria in 1901, at the height of Britain's imperial power, the most that even the most liberal politician would contemplate was some kind of weak dominion status for the still-troublesome Irish. Even that seemed far away until the general

John Redmond
(Mercier Archive)

election of 1910 left the Irish Parliamentary Party (IPP), led by John Redmond, holding the balance of power in the Liberal government's coalition. Redmond demanded Home Rule for Ireland in return for his party's support, and in 1912 the British prime minister, Herbert Henry Asquith, introduced the third Home Rule Bill to the House of Commons, which, if passed into law, would once again give Ireland its own parliament, albeit one with restricted powers.

The reaction of the unionists in the north was immediate. The UVF was established to oppose the introduction of Home Rule, by force if necessary, and on 28 September the Solemn League and Covenant was signed by nearly half a million unionists pledging to oppose the measure. By failing to take a strong stance against this, partly due to the refusal of senior military officers to take up

Ulster's Solemn League and Covenant.

Being convinced in our consciences that Home Rule would be disastrous to the material well-being of Ulster as well as of the whole of Ireland, subversive of our civil and religious freedom, destructive of our citizenship and perilous to the unity of the Empire, we, whose names are underwritten, men of Ulster, loyal subjects of His Gracious Majesty King George V., humbly relying on the God whom our fathers in days of stress and trial confidently trusted, do hereby pledge ourselves in solemn Covenant throughout this our time of threatened calamity to stand by one another in defending for ourselves and our children our cherished position of equal citizenship in the United Kingdom and in using all means which may be found necessary to defeat the present conspiracy to set up a Home Rule Parliament in Ireland. And in the event of such a Parliament being forced upon us we further solemnly and mutually pledge ourselves to refuse to recognise its authority. In sure confidence that God will defend the right we hereto subscribe our names. And further, we individually declare that we have not already signed this Covenant.

The above was signed by me at_____
"Ulster Day," Saturday, 28th September, 1912,

God Save the King.

The Solemn League and Covenant.
(Mercier Archive)

arms against the unionists, the British government essentially doomed Home Rule from the start.

The First World War – and the 1916 Easter Rising – changed everything. At the start of the war Home Rule was effectively postponed until the conflict was over. John Redmond encouraged the Irish Volunteers to join the British in the fight against Germany and many chose to do so, leaving the organisation with much smaller numbers, but more republican ideals. They embraced the principle of 'England's difficulty = Ireland's opportunity' and took their chance during Easter Week 1916, rising up against the British. Although it failed militarily, the Rising shook the British government.

Though conscious that Ireland was now the focus of much world attention, especially from America, British politicians, even Liberals such as Asquith, made no attempt to conceal their distaste for the nationalist demand for an Irish Republic so publicly announced during the Rising. What increased these politicians' spleen and blunted their normal political acumen was their need to continue a war they were not winning and which was already costing an enormous number of lives. They saw the Rising as heinously disloyal, and crushed it without mercy, executing the Dublin leadership and imprisoning

Henry Street, Dublin, after the Rising. (Mercier Archive)

a multitude of men, many of whom had played no part in the rebellion, as well as a small number of women. These actions only served to garner greater support for the Volunteers both nationally and internationally.

In December 1916 an amnesty for those imprisoned after the Rising was announced and the majority returned in triumph to Ireland. The Volunteers recovered quickly, and in some parts of the country, particularly Munster, the continuity of arming and public drilling soon brought nationalists into conflict with the police and the army. Insensitivity or bloody-mindedness on the part of the British government, which was harried by demands from the generals for more soldiers, sharply increased anti-British feeling.

On 30 September 1917 the funeral of Thomas Ashe was the occasion of the largest nationalist demonstration seen since Daniel O'Connell's monster meeting at Tara in 1843. Ashe was the hero of the Volunteers' most successful action during Easter Week, the battle of Ashbourne. He was arrested in July 1917 for allegedly make seditious comments, and incarcerated in Mountjoy

The firing party at the grave of Thomas Ashe.
(Courtesy of Kilmainham Gaol Museum,
KMGLM 2018.0058)

Prison in Dublin. As a result of injuries inflicted on him during a botched force-feeding while he was on hunger strike, he died on 25 September.

The proposal in April 1918 to apply conscription to Ireland, followed by the appointment of the hard-line Sir John French as lord lieutenant in May 1918, amounted almost to an incitement to rebellion. The new British prime minister, David Lloyd George, tried to mitigate the unpopularity of the proposed conscription by offering the immediate implementation of the Home Rule terms that had been agreed before the war. This offer was manifestly insincere, since it had no unionist support and by now promised too little to have any persuasive force for the majority of the country.

David Lloyd George
(Mercier Archive)

An announcement, made about a week later by French, that Sinn Féin was in league with the Germans was widely derided, but it led, on 17–18 May, to the arrest of a hundred leading republicans, including Éamon de Valera, the highest ranking survivor of the Volunteers after the Rising, and Arthur Griffith. Griffith was

Éamon de Valera
(Mercier Archive)

Arthur Griffith
(Mercier Archive)

the founder of Sinn Féin, a political party which proposed that Ireland should be an equal partner with Britain in a dual monarchy under the English crown. (The Irish words *sinn féin* mean 'ourselves'.) The means of obtaining this goal were to be passive resistance and the setting up of alternative institutions to the existing British ones. This approach met with little practical success, but its ideas were wrongly assumed by the authorities to be the philosophical basis for the Easter Rising. By linking the party so closely to the Rising, the British actually reinvigorated Sinn Féin, and it soon came to be the main party of the Volunteers.

The effect of the threat of conscription and the arrests linked to the so-called 'German Plot' was to unite nationalist Ireland as never before and to shift the balance of power away from the parliamentary nationalists to the militants. The anti-conscription campaign was fought by all nationalist groups, with the strong support of the Catholic Church and the trade unions. The measure (and the promise of Home Rule) was eventually dropped on 20 June, by which time many counties in the west and south were, on French's instructions, under at least partial martial law.

In December 1918, following the end of the First World War, a general election was held and the results were significant, not only in Ireland – where Sinn Féin secured 73 out of 105 Irish seats and the IPP, now led by John Dillon (1851–1927), a mere 6 – but also in Westminster, where Lloyd George was returned as head of a coalition dependent on the Conservatives, led by Andrew Bonar Law. The latter had promised total

Andrew Bonar Law
(Courtesy of the Library of Congress, LC-DIG-ggbain-23420)

support for Ulster's unionists as early as 1912 and now he left Lloyd George with little room to manoeuvre in Ireland. Moreover, the victory of Sinn Féin all but signalled the death knell for any chance that Home Rule would still be acceptable to the majority of the Irish. The sides had polarised and conflict seemed inevitable.

Yet, though the nationalists would have liked to take the Sinn Féin electoral victory as a licence to proceed with a military campaign, many party members had not given up the hope of a constitutional settlement. The party was even regarded among the ordinary people as the best insurance against renewed violence.

Some of the newly elected parliamentarians, particularly de Valera, pinned their hopes on the Paris Peace Conference, which was due to open on 18 January 1919 to consider the rights of 'small nations'. The dominating figure at the conference was to be the American president, Woodrow Wilson (1856–1924). It was assumed that Wilson, as a Democrat, would be sympathetic to nationalist aspirations, but given the resolute Presbyterianism of his County Tyrone grandparents and his own instinctive Waspishness, this proved incorrect. He was clearly reluctant to do anything about a matter that the British delegation insisted was 'internal'.

With the conclusion of the peace talks and the signing of the Treaty of Versailles in June 1919, the British once again turned their attention to the 'Irish problem'. However, the reaction of the British establishment to the Ulster unionists in 1912 had heralded an unassailable problem. Unwilling or unable to force this minority to work with an Irish government, it was now proposed to split the country under two governments – one for the northern six counties (Antrim, Armagh, Derry, Down, Fermanagh and Tyrone) and one for the other twenty-six. The resulting partition, which was signed into British law by the Government of Ireland Act in 1920, created a state with a built-in unionist majority and a pervasive condition of second-class citizenship for the three-quarters of a million nationalists whose homes were in Northern Ireland, as the six counties were termed. (The considerable unionist populations of Donegal, Monaghan and Cavan were excluded.)

The remaining twenty-six counties had been offered such a diluted 'independence' that the words 'home rule' were risible.

It is tempting to think that, because things happened the way they did, no other outcome was possible. In fact there were other prospects for a possible peaceful solution, but a number of the people on the nationalist side, including Dan Breen and Seán Treacy, were convinced that nothing but a resort to arms would bring the British to their senses. It was an old argument, but in this case there existed the will and the means to carry it out – and so the War of Independence began.

The country which had in general mocked, where it did not deplore, the 1916 rebels, now found itself countenancing much greater violence and tolerating what, a little earlier, it would have regarded as criminal. The leaders of the Irish Republican Army (the new name

Cathal Brugha
(Mercier Archive)

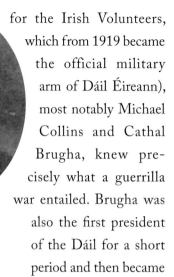

Michael Collins
(Courtesy of
Chrissy Osborne)

for the Irish Volunteers, which from 1919 became the official military arm of Dáil Éireann), most notably Michael Collins and Cathal Brugha, knew precisely what a guerrilla war entailed. Brugha was also the first president of the Dáil for a short period and then became minister for defence from April 1919 to August 1921. Collins, who had little experience of politics (though he was learning fast), was initially named minister for home affairs and then minister for finance. He knew that, in a country where people were sent to prison for singing seditious songs or giving their names in Irish when accosted by policemen, and where there were already easily mobilised local bands of armed Volunteers, a war could be started. What he was not sure of was whether people realised what such a war would mean on the ground.

The War of Independence was an often squalid and violent affair, as is inevitably the case with such struggles: participants ruthlessly acted out the logic of their aims; gallantry to defeated enemies was, with rare exceptions, unknown on either side; and reprisals were often out of all proportion to the original events that had triggered them. Though called a war of independence, the conflict's primary purpose – to gain independence for the entire island of Ireland – was rendered *de facto* unachievable with the partitioning of the country by the Government of Ireland Act in 1920. Any victory obtained by a continuation of the war would therefore be incomplete.

By the time the war started, life tended to be regarded as cheap: had not millions, including approximately 40,000 Irish nationals, been killed in the First World War? Those involved in the guerrilla war – mainly young men – found it necessary to stifle normal human feelings; these emotions finally found their outlet in incredulous dismay at the savagery of their opponents and in self-exculpatory accounts, both oral and written, composed by participants on both sides long after the actual events. On the Volunteers' side, ancient rage and revenge often initiated violence against 'innocents' who were perceived as being 'on the other side', and the war was used to settle personal grudges as well as to ease an atavistic sense of injustice. The crown forces, especially the newly created 'Black and Tans' and the even more ruthless Auxiliary Division, treated the whole Irish population as hostile, and many unarmed civilians were killed in cold blood.

Volunteer tactics required British repression for them to garner support, and for the next three

Shops burned by British forces as a reprisal in Mallow, County Cork. (Mercier Archive)

years the IRA and the security forces were in an ironic way collaborators. Ambushes followed by disproportionate reprisals; expressions of national cultural and political will frustrated by draconian oppression; the reputation of both police and army besmirched by gross breaches of discipline – all increased support for violent tactics.

When the Dáil met for the first time on 21 January in the Mansion House in Dawson Street, Dublin, it was not realised by many that the war for independence had already started. But even though the actions of Breen, Treacy and their small group of Tipperary Volunteers forced the new government's hand, all members were determined from the outset that this time, unlike all the previous attempts to free Ireland from Britain's tyranny, they would succeed, no matter the cost.

RESORT TO ARMS

SEÁN TREACY, one of the leaders of the Soloheadbeg ambush, had initiated the war for independence because, as he put it, 'it was high time we did a bit of pushing'. Dan Breen, who also took part, gave a different version of events: 'The Volunteers were in great danger of becoming merely a political adjunct to the Sinn Féin organisation.' The nine participants were mostly local: both Breen and Treacy lived close to the quarry to which the 168 pounds of gelignite and thirty-eight detonators were being conveyed by horse and cart from the military barracks in Tipperary. Two RIC constables, fifty-seven-year-old James McDonnell, a married man from County Mayo, and thirty-six-year-old Patrick O'Connell, a bachelor from County Cork, were sent along as guards with the driver, Edward

Godfrey, and county council employee Patrick Flynn. When challenged by the Volunteers, the constables moved to draw their weapons. Treacy and his men opened fire, and the RIC men fell dead in a hail of rifle and revolver shots. However, as Breen leaped over a gateway to collect the policemen's rifles and the gelignite, the mask he was wearing slipped, thus enabling his identification. The authorities were able to use his photograph on reward posters offering £1,000 for information leading to his capture (see opposite).

Though Soloheadbeg was the first action in the struggle, it shared one feature with similar later attacks: local intelligence was of good quality. The South Tipperary Brigade had been told that a consignment of explosives would 'soon be on its way to the quarry' and so every day from 16 January the ambush party was in position, from dawn to around 2 p.m. in the afternoon, until the actual day of the ambush.

Local and national reaction was one of condemnation. The constables had been popular members of a small-town community; a relief fund for McDonnell's family (he left a wife and

POLICE NOTICE.

£1000 REWARD

WANTED FOR MURDER IN IRELAND.

DANIEL BREEN

(calls himself Commandant of the Third
Tipperary Brigade).

Age 27, 5 feet 7 inches in height, bronzed complexion, dark hair (long in front), grey eyes, short cocked nose, stout build, weight about 12 stone, clean shaven; sulky bulldog appearance; looks rather like a blacksmith coming from work; wears cap pulled well down over face.

(Mercier Archive)

five children) was set up immediately. The local clergy and Dr Harty, the archbishop of Cashel, declared the action morally wrong. It was also condemned by Sinn Féin and leading members of the Irish Republican Brotherhood (IRB), though whether their disapproval was because of the action itself or simply because they hadn't approved it is unclear. Certainly *An tÓglach*, the IRA's official publication during the war edited by Piaras Béaslaí, announced on 31 January that Volunteers were morally and politically entitled to inflict death on the enemies of the state: soldiers and policemen of the British government.

The next RIC casualty was Constable Martin O'Brien, who was shot on 6 April during an attempt to rescue Robert Byrne, adjutant of the Limerick City 2nd Battalion of the IRA, from the Union Hospital. Byrne had been imprisoned in January and had later gone on hunger strike. The authorities, loath to risk force-feeding after the Ashe debacle, had him moved to hospital when his condition deteriorated. Having been shot during the rescue, Byrne himself died later that evening.

Like south Tipperary after Soloheadbeg and Westport after the shooting of a magistrate on the night of 29 March, Limerick was quickly proclaimed a special military area. Though all these deaths had initially been greeted mainly with revulsion, the swamping of the areas with military and police checkpoints, the humiliating body searches, the requirement of permits for journeys or even the driving of stock to market, and the general interference with ordinary life that such a status brought, soon blunted the regret. It seemed that the British government had learned nothing, not even the wisdom of allowing the local and generally tactful RIC to continue to maintain order.

Seán Hogan
(Mercier Archive)

The Soloheadbeg team was in action once again on 13 May. Seán Hogan of the 3rd Tipperary Brigade was being transported to prison in Cork on the Thurles to Cork train when he was rescued by Treacy, Breen and their men at Knocklong Station, just over the county boundary in Limerick. As a result of the action, Sergeant Peter Wallace and Constable Michael Enright died from gunshot wounds, and Breen himself was so severely wounded that he was not expected to survive. Again there was strong condemnation of the shootings, with Dr Harty denouncing the action and urging Irishmen 'not to stain the fair name of their native land with deeds of blood'.

In all, fifteen policemen were killed in 1919, including District Inspector Michael Hunt, who was shot after the Thurles Races on 23 June. Of those who lost their lives, two were DMP detectives: Detective Sergeant Patrick Smyth (killed on 30 July) and Detective Constable Daniel Hoey (12 September). They were part of the DMP's detective division, known as G Division. Its members were called 'G-men' long before the members of J. Edgar Hoover's FBI became known by the same name. What is particularly significant about their deaths was the fact that they were the first victims of Collins' deadly band

Daniel Hoey (the tall man at the back) was shot outside police headquarters in Brunswick Street. In the centre with the moustache is DS Smyth, who was shot on 30 July 1919.
(Mercier Archive)

of counter-intelligence operatives known as 'the Squad'.

DS Smyth was a very effective detective, known as 'Dog' Smyth because of his sleuthing abilities. Collins had a number of G-men, including Smyth, warned against their involvement in intelligence work, but Smyth persisted. On the night he was killed, five gunmen lay in wait for him and shot him when he alighted from a tram at Drumcondra Bridge near his home. Despite being hit a number of times, with the help of his children he reached his house before collapsing. He died later, in the Mater hospital.

DC Hoey had been an intended target of Collins ever since 1916, when he identified Seán Mac Diarmada (1884–1916), one of the leaders of the Rising, in a crowd of Volunteers waiting to be shipped to the relative safety of an English prison. Mac Diarmada was executed in Kilmainham Gaol on 12 May 1916 and the name of Hoey was filed away in Collins' prodigious memory for future action. He was shot as he entered the police station in Brunswick Street on the day that the British government proscribed Dáil Éireann.

Collins was enough of a student of Irish history to realise that in all previous Irish insurrections – that of the United Irishmen in 1798, Robert Emmet's in 1803, William Smith O'Brien's in 1848 and the Fenian outbreak in 1867 – British government intelligence agents had discovered the details of plans and personnel

Some members of the Squad (l to r): Michael McDonnell, Tom Keogh, Vincent Byrne, Paddy O'Daly and James Slattery.
(Mercier Archive)

well in advance of the attack. He was determined to reverse this situation by building up his own network of spies and counter-intelligence operatives. The Squad was essentially a band of expert gunmen officially formed in September 1919, though a notional group existed before that. Dick McKee, one of Collins' chief aides, who helped train the Squad, had warned prospective members that those with scruples about taking a life should not join.

One of Collins' most effective intelligence operatives was Eamon 'Ned' Broy. He had joined the DMP in 1911 and was a detective sergeant serving as a clerk in G Division when he offered his services to Collins. His usual technique was to make an extra copy of every document he dealt with and pass that copy by various means to Collins. It was from Broy that Collins got the list of those whom the British government intended to arrest under the pretext of the 'German Plot'. As a result, Collins was able to warn de Valera and the rest of the Volunteer Executive, the controlling body of the Volunteers, at their meeting on 17 May 1918 that they were likely to be arrested. For some reason de Valera went home; a few days later he found himself a prisoner in Lincoln Jail. His rescue from that prison on 3 February 1919 became part of the Collins legend, with all the ripping-yarns paraphernalia of keys made from wax impressions which broke in the lock, and the prisoner walking arm in arm with one of his rescuers past groups of courting Tommies and their sweethearts.

At this time de Valera was the obvious leader

of the Irish forces: he was a veteran of Easter Week and a politician with a remarkably supple, not to say Machiavellian, mind. Indeed, he was famous for recommending that Richard Mulcahy, the Volunteer chief of staff, read Machiavelli's *Il Principe* (*The Prince*). However, ever since the Rising he had shown a distrust of violence. After his escape from Lincoln, rather than stay at home to organise the war that was brewing, he instead insisted on going to America to raise support for the recognition of Ireland as an independent state. This decision caused the rest of the Dáil Executive, of which he was president, some dismay, especially those like Griffith (released in a general amnesty in March) who wished to hold the militants in check.

De Valera's absence left Collins largely free to conduct the war as he saw fit. He knew the propaganda and morale-boosting value of the 'spectacular' to complement the series of raids and ambushes being carried out by individual IRA brigades across the country, and it seemed to him that the most spectacular action might be the successful assassination of the lord lieutenant and

Martin Savage
(Mercier Archive)

viceroy, Sir John French. On 19 December 1919 French, who had been visiting his ancestral estate at Frenchpark in Roscommon, was on his way back to Dublin. An ambush was laid near the viceregal lodge in the Phoenix Park, but the only casualty was a Volunteer named Martin Savage, who was killed in the crossfire. After the *Irish Independent* described Savage as 'a would-be assassin' on 21 December, the paper's offices and presses were destroyed by a party of IRA men.

As well as being virtual commander of operations by this point, Collins was also minister for finance in the Dáil, and he raised nearly £380,000 in redeemable bonds repayable by the future independent Ireland.

Although the Irish campaign started off slowly

*Collins at the steps of St Enda's school, established by 1916
leader Patrick Pearse, signing republican bonds on the block
upon which Robert Emmet, leader of the 1803 rebellion, had
been beheaded.* (Mercier Archive)

in 1919, by the end of the year it had become increasingly organised. Sinn Féin controlled so many county councils that they were largely able to take control of the government of local areas. Rates were no longer paid to the British tax office and republican arbitration courts, the decisions of which were binding, were preferred to official state ones. There was even a republican police force set up. This 'dry run' at self-government increased confidence sufficiently that post-Treaty Ireland was governed with unexpected efficiency. Meanwhile, the RIC and their families were being subjected to a countrywide policy of ostracism, which had led to a significant drop in morale, and were increasingly dependent on military support. The signs were not good for continued British rule in Ireland in 1920.

THE BRITISH FIGHT BACK

THE new year saw an increase in IRA attacks on the struggling RIC across the country. With its local knowledge, this police force was viewed by the IRA as Britain's most effective weapon in Ireland. From just fifteen the previous year, the number of RIC dead in 1920 would eventually reach 179. Not surprisingly this led to an increase in resignations and a drop in native recruits. The numbers who had left the force in 1919 for all causes was around 495, of which only 99 had resigned. The equivalent figures for 1920 were 3,229, with over half that number resignations. As a result March saw the ominous arrival of the first members of a new group of recruits from Britain who were intended to supplement the native Irish force.

The order for supplementary recruitment

was issued in January 1920. The new personnel were largely ex-soldiers and ex-sailors who, unemployed and finding life difficult after the end of the First World War, were happy to become mercenaries for ten shillings a day and all-found. These new recruits were urgently needed, but the first group arrived so precipitously that complete uniforms could not be found for them. Dark-green RIC uniforms had to be supplemented with khaki military uniforms. It is thought that when the new members of the force first appeared on patrol in County Tipperary, where there was a

Members of the RIC and Black and Tans at Midleton Barracks, County Cork. (Mercier Archive)

famous local pack of hounds called the 'Black and Tans', the name was applied to the new recruits because of their appearance and, although the deficiencies in the uniform were sorted out by the end of 1920, it stuck. In spite of the equally foul reputation of the Auxiliary Division, who were first recruited in July 1920 to further supplement the RIC, the struggle of 1920–21 became commonly known as the 'Tan war'.

In spite of contemporary belief, the vetting process at recruitment for the Tans was nearly as strict as for ordinary RIC officers. There may have been some who had a criminal record, but most were ordinary young men who turned out to be only too happy to engage in the reprisals that were at first secretly condoned and eventually openly approved by the increasingly desperate authorities. The 'sweepings of English jails' – the usual nationalist jibe aimed at the Tans – was an inaccurate description, yet many of the exploits of the new recruits were criminal if viewed in absolute terms. They were badly trained and, apart from the perhaps one-quarter of them who were Irish recruits, had no experience or knowledge of the country in which they found themselves. Even the Irish recruits, who were mainly of Ulster origin, would have found Munster and west Connacht, the main places of deployment outside of Dublin, somewhat alien.

Despite their reputation, it was not the Tans who perpetrated the first serious breach of police discipline in the war. In fact, this took place in Thurles before they were mobilised. On 22 January 1920 twenty-nine-year-old Constable Michael Finnegan was walking home to the Mall when he was shot by three men. The local police immediately went on a rampage, shooting out windows in the premises of twelve prominent Sinn Féiners and throwing grenades through the office window of the *Tipperary Star*.

Worse was to come. On the night of 19–20 March, after the shooting of Constable Joseph Murtagh on Pope's Quay, Cork, a band of armed men with blackened faces and in civilian clothes surrounded the home of Tomás MacCurtain, the Sinn Féin lord mayor of the city and commandant of Cork No. 1 Brigade of the IRA, and demanded entry. When MacCurtain's wife opened the door,

Tomás MacCurtain
(Mercier Archive)

two of them rushed straight upstairs and shot him at point blank range. The inquest into his death returned a verdict of wilful murder against 'David Lloyd George, Prime Minister of England, Lord French, Lord Lieutenant of Ireland, Ian MacPherson, late Chief Secretary of Ireland, Acting Inspector General Smith of the RIC, Divisional Inspector Clayton of the RIC, DI Swanzy and some unknown members of the RIC'.

Although the authorities tried to blame the killing on members of the IRA, who they claimed were impatient at MacCurtain's lack of action, no one believed that story. Following the attack, DI Oswald Swanzy was placed on Collins' list of enemies to be eliminated, and he was shot in Lisburn, County Antrim, on 22 August, where he had been moved after the inquest's verdict was

The funeral procession of Tomás MacCurtain in Cork city.
(Mercier Archive)

made public. The aftermath of Swanzy's death was serious sectarian rioting in Lisburn and Belfast. Most Catholic houses in Lisburn were destroyed and there were twenty-four civilian deaths. These riots, together with even more savage ones in Derry earlier in the summer, led to the recruitment in November of that year of the Ulster Special Constabulary. Made up of 'A', 'B' and 'C' Specials, it was the 'B' Specials who would gain particular notoriety as a violent partisan force whose reign of terror over the nationalist community lasted until their final disbandment in 1970.

The shock of MacCurtain's death and the evidence of RIC involvement in the murder was overshadowed somewhat by the Squad's killing of Alan Bell on 26 March. Bell was an elderly magistrate who was part of Lord French's counter-espionage team. Known to have been successful in finding evidence of Sinn Féin bank accounts, he travelled by tram each day from his home in Monkstown to his office in Dublin Castle without a guard. That morning four members of the Squad took him off the tram at Ballsbridge and shot him. This was a further serious blow to the morale of British forces in the city, which had already been severely tested by the Squad's killing of William Redmond, the assistant commissioner of the DMP, in January. Redmond, who had been put in charge of the demoralised G Division, was shot as he walked from the Castle to his hotel in Harcourt Street.

Another high-profile incident had a less

bloody conclusion. General Cuthbert Henry Tindall Lucas, who commanded military forces in Cork and Tipperary, was captured by an IRA platoon led by Liam Lynch while fishing on the Blackwater, near Fermoy, County Cork, on 26 July. He was moved around for a month until his guard, Michael Brennan, tired of supplying him with a daily bottle of whiskey paid for out of Brennan's own pocket, allowed him to escape.

General Lucas being held captive by his IRA guards. Left to right: P. Brennan, Paddy Brennan, General Lucas, Michael Brennan and Joe Keane. (Mercier Archive)

Relations between the general and his captors were genial; he played tennis, made hay and wrote and received daily letters to and from his wife. They took him salmon poaching one night and he was relieved to see that the IRA boat-

Liam Lynch
(Mercier Archive)

man was the river bailiff. On the darker side, the general's troops went on the rampage in Fermoy and other towns in reprisal for the kidnapping, although, unlike in Tan and Auxiliary raids, no one was killed.

The Auxiliary Division of the RIC – its members were commonly known as Auxies – was the brainchild of Winston Churchill, secretary of state for war and air in Lloyd George's post-war government coalition. The Auxies were made up of ex-British Army officers and were given the rank of cadet. Initially they wore army uniforms, with distinctive Glengarry bonnets. Later they

Members of F Company of the Auxiliary Division at the Mansion House in Dublin. (Mercier Archive)

changed their uniform to one of a blue colour with black chest bandoliers and leather belts holding bayonets and open holsters with .45 revolvers, but they retained the caps. Most had been high-ranking officers and many had been decorated for valour; their ranks included two holders of the VC as well as many DSOs, MCs and holders of the *Croix de Guerre*. Their reputation in Ireland, however, was one of drunkenness, brutality and lack of discipline, to the extent that their commander, General Frank Crozier, resigned on 19 February 1921, less than a year after taking command.

The Auxies were conceived as quick-response, motorised units of a hundred men whose targets were the newly organised IRA flying columns, which operated mainly in

Brig. Gen. Frank Crozier
(Mercier Archive)

Munster. Amongst their most notorious actions were the 'sackings' of various Irish towns. Typical was what happened in Balbriggan, County Dublin, on the night of 20 September 1920. Head Constable Peter Burke and his brother Michael, a sergeant, were shot with dum-dum bullets in a public house. Peter died immediately, although Michael later recovered from his wounds. Peter had been involved in training the Auxiliary Division in the Phoenix Park RIC depot in Dublin. A party of Auxiliaries arrived

Balbriggan after its sacking by Auxiliaries.
(Courtesy of Kilmainham Gaol Museum, 19PC-1A46-25)

The Auxiliaries sometimes used bloodhounds to try to track IRA men. (Mercier Archive)

from Gormanston and, it is said, on seeing their old instructor lying dead, wreaked destruction on local properties with grenades, setting many houses on fire and savagely killing two civilians with bayonets. The scene was marked by lines of refugees fleeing from their ravaged town.

As the policy of reprisals became commonplace, it became the practice of the beleaguered inhabitants of towns and villages where reprisals were expected to leave their homes at sundown and spend the night in what safety they could find in hedges and barns. Similar scenes to those of Balbriggan followed the ambush of a police patrol at Rineen, between Miltown Malbay and Lahinch, County Clare, on 22 September. Five constables were killed outright (one managed to crawl away from the scene and his body was only discovered the following day), while their sergeant died of his wounds on 24 September. Houses were burned in nearby towns and four people were killed, including one who tried to help a neighbour put out the fire in his house.

A few days later, it was the turn of Trim, County Meath, when the town was wrecked and the shops looted by Tans after the RIC barracks was set on fire by the IRA. The next day, during a raid on the RIC barracks in Mallow, County Cork, led by Liam Lynch and Ernie O'Malley, an army sergeant was killed, and later that evening the army ravaged the town. The worst of the violence, however, was yet to come.

Ernie O'Malley
(Mercier Archive)

THE VIOLENCE ESCALATES

THE AUTUMN of 1920 was characterised by attacks on RIC barracks, now fortified by barbed wire and sandbags, as well as ambushes, reprisals and counter-reprisals, intimidation and physical violence inflicted on civilians by both sides. The cities of Cork, Limerick and Dublin, and the counties of Cork, Tipperary, Kerry, Limerick, Clare, Roscommon and Donegal bore the brunt of the fighting. Yet even there, large areas were unaffected, except by dread and rumour, and the inconvenience of military restrictions.

The number of fatalities among the RIC increased dramatically during the second half of the year. And though official sanction for reprisals for attacks on British forces was not given until January 1921, there was little attempt made to investigate those responsible for the indiscriminate killing of civilians during such actions. After Balbriggan, Sir Hamar Greenwood, the chief secretary for Ireland, who had been appointed on 4 April 1920 and whose public utterances became so specious that 'telling a Hamar' became a euphemism for lying, told the House of Commons that it was 'impossible' to find out who was responsible for the burning, looting and killing.

On 19 June the willingness of the upper echelons of the British forces to use whatever means necessary to crush their opponents was baldly stated by Lieutenant Colonel Gerald Brice Smyth, the RIC divisional police commissioner for Munster, when he addressed a group of RIC officers in Listowel Barracks. Smyth urged the policemen to be ruthless and suggested that there would be no consequences for killing

Lt Col Brice Smyth
(Mercier Archive)

Sir Hamar Greenwood inspecting members of the Auxiliaries in Dublin. (Mercier Archive)

the innocent: 'The more you shoot the better I will like you, and no policeman will get into trouble for shooting a man.' He also hinted at the vicious treatment that was being meted out to IRA prisoners and proclaimed, since the aim was to wipe out 'Sinn Féin': 'Any man who is not prepared to co-operate is a hindrance rather than a help and he had better leave the force at once.'

When Smyth had finished, one courageous constable, Jeremiah Mee, walked up to the table and threw his revolver and cap upon it, saying

Jeremiah Mee
(Courtesy of
J. Anthony Gaughan)

that Smyth's speech was an incitement to murder. When Smyth ordered his arrest, it quickly became clear that Mee had the support of his fellow police officers and Smyth was forced to make a hasty retreat. The incident became known as the 'Listowel Mutiny'.

As a result of his speech, the highly decorated, one-armed army veteran Smyth was added to Collins' list for assassination. He was killed in the smoking-room of the Cork County Club on 17 July by members of Cork No. 1 Brigade. Constable Mee and several of his colleagues resigned on 6 July and Mee was soon recruited by Countess Markievicz for a bureau set up to help members of the RIC who were dismissed or had resigned.

Major George Smyth, who was then serving in Egypt, on hearing of the death of his brother Gerald applied for a transfer to Irish intelligence, bringing with him, it is said, eleven comrades for the sole intention of avenging the killing, which he blamed, incorrectly, on Dan Breen. Breen and Seán Treacy had been active in Dublin since the failed attempt on Lord French's life in which they had taken part; they were doughty fighters and Collins wanted to keep them under his direct control.

The arrival of Smyth in Dublin coincided with the effective reorganisation of British intelligence by Brigadier General Sir Ormonde de l'Épée Winter, known to the Squad as the 'Holy

Sir Ormonde de l'Épée Winter, chief of British intelligence in Dublin Castle. (Mercier Archive)

Terror'. His agents had discovered that Breen and another man, who turned out to be Treacy, were holed up in a safe house in Drumcondra owned by Professor John Carolan of St Patrick's Training College. On the evening of 11 October Winter's men, including Smyth, raided the house. In the shoot-out that followed, Smyth and another officer, Captain A. P. White, were fatally wounded, while Treacy and Breen managed to escape, although both were wounded, Breen severely. After they took control of the house, the British put Carolan up against a wall and shot him in the head. He died the next day.

The funeral procession of Smyth and White, fixed for 14 October, was expected to be a solemn affair, and it was thought that General Nevil Macready (British commander-in-chief since April) and General Henry Tudor (commander of the RIC) would be among the mourners. It was too good an opportunity for Collins to miss. The Squad, with Treacy among them, attended, but the generals did not, probably on Winter's advice. That same day Treacy was recognised in the doorway of the Republican Outfitters on Talbot Street, run by Dublin IRA officer

General Henry Hugh Tudor
(Mercier Archive)

Peadar Clancy, and was killed during a shoot-out with British intelligence agents.

Two other 'names' of IRA mythology were to die that autumn: Terence MacSwiney, who had succeeded Tomás MacCurtain as lord mayor of Cork, died on 25 October after seventy-four days on hunger strike; and Kevin Barry, an eighteen-year-old medical student and IRA member, was hanged after being captured in possession of a gun at the scene of an ambush where a young soldier was killed. Barry's execution bequeathed us one of the best-known ballads of the period, which includes the lines: 'Another martyr for old Ireland; another murder for the crown'.

The deaths of both men increased the surge of international opposition to what Britain was doing in Ireland. The *Manchester Guardian* and

Terence MacSwiney
(Mercier Archive)

Kevin Barry (Courtesy of Kilmainham Gaol Museum, 19PC-1A46-17)

*The funeral procession of Terence MacSwiney in London had
a guard of honour of Volunteers in prohibited uniform and the
streets were filled with mourners, not all of them Irish exiles.*
(Mercier Archive)

the *Daily News* (whose literary editor, Robert
Lynd, had been an early member of Sinn Féin
and a friend of Roger Casement, executed for his
role in seeking German support for the Rising)
attacked the British government constantly, effectively neutralising the rabid anti-Irish propaganda
of English publications such as the *Morning Post*
and the *Spectator*.

The most effective propaganda sheet was the *Irish Bulletin*, put out by Desmond FitzGerald (1889–1947), Frank Gallagher and Erskine Childers. The *Bulletin* had even more impact abroad than at home. Its experienced journalists – Childers had written the bestselling *The Riddle of the Sands* (1903), which anticipated Germany's entry into the First World War – were able to depict IRA successes as heroic, while condemning the actions of British forces as squalidly savage. As a result of such publicity, de Valera was able to win a great deal of sympathy in America for the Irish cause – as well as securing $5 million for use in Ireland.

The bloodiest month of 1920 proved to be November. At the start of this month, Lloyd George was clearly out to please his audience when he claimed at the yearly Guildhall banquet in the City of London on 9 November, that 'We have murder by the throat' in Ireland. He used the occasion to exonerate those crown forces guilty of excesses in Ireland and hinted that they should be given a freer rein in the future. This hint of an official sanction for reprisals and the treating of the IRA as criminals was also to please Winston Churchill, who, though a Liberal, was by this time giving clear indications of his intention to rejoin the Conservative Party from which he had defected in 1904. It was Churchill who had insisted that Kevin Barry be hanged as a murderer, prompting J. H. Thomas, afterwards secretary of state for the colonies in Ramsay MacDonald's first Labour government, to condemn the execution in the House of Commons.

Lloyd George's words were promptly disproved when, in the early morning of 21 November, the Squad killed twelve men thought to be members of the British intelligence service in their homes and hotels. Two Auxiliaries, Frank Garniss and Cecil Morris, who happened to be passing the scene of one of the killings in Lower Mount Street and were sent for reinforcements, were also killed. Two of Collins' closest aides, Dick McKee and Peadar Clancy, who had been arrested the previous evening, along with Conor Clune, a civilian who had been caught up in the arrests, were 'shot while trying to escape' in Dublin Castle.

A group of British intelligence officers who were working in Dublin in 1920. This photograph was in possession of the IRA, who numbered the men, presumably for identification purposes. (Mercier Archive)

So began 'Bloody Sunday'. It was the day of a Gaelic football match between Dublin and Tipperary, and Croke Park was crowded that afternoon. The grounds were surrounded by crown forces, who anticipated that there would be IRA men among the spectators. A party of Auxiliaries drove into the ground while the match was in progress. Predictably, they later claimed they had been fired on from the crowd. Whether or not this was true, what is certain is that they turned their guns on the stands and the teams. Fourteen people died – some from bullets, others trampled to death as the hysterical crowd tried to find cover. The fatalities included a woman, a ten-year-old boy and one of the Tipperary forwards.

These events received worldwide publicity, and gave further impetus to secret truce negotiations that had been going on since October and were now led by Griffith. However, these efforts were frustrated when Griffith was arrested on 26 November.

Despite their losses on Bloody Sunday, worse was to come for the British that month. On Sunday 28 November Tom Barry's West Cork flying column ambushed a patrol of Auxiliaries at Kilmichael. Flying columns were small groups of men, generally on the run, who moved from place to place, their mobility allowing them to strike at the enemy wherever they found a suitable opportunity. Barry's was one of the most effective of these units. The Auxiliary cadets they ambushed that November were under the command of DI F. W. Crake and were travelling in

Tom Barry
(Mercier Archive)

two Crossley tenders on their usual triangular sweep: Macroom, Dunmanway, Bandon and back to Macroom. Barry chose a stretch of bogland near Kilmichael, eight miles from Macroom, for his attack. By the end of the action seventeen Auxiliaries lay dead. Cadet Guthrie, who managed to escape the ambush, was caught later, attempting to make his way back to Macroom, and executed. Only one Auxiliary survived, and only because he was so badly wounded that the IRA thought he was dead. After the attack there were accusations that the IRA had mutilated the bodies of the dead using axes, although the post mortem results appear to rule this out, and it was also insisted by the British government that some of their men were killed after they had surrendered. However, Barry claimed that during the fight the Auxiliaries only pretended to surrender, and then treacherously opened fire again once the IRA showed themselves, which resulted in the deaths of two of his men. He lost three men in total.

A reprisal, perhaps the most notorious of all, came two weeks later, on the night of Saturday 11 December. That evening another ambush was carried out on an Auxiliary patrol, this time at Dillon's Cross in Cork city. Eleven of the Auxiliaries were wounded, one of whom would die the following day. A few hours after this ambush the centre of the city was set on fire by a combined force of Tans and Auxiliaries. They prevented the fire service from reaching the sites of many of the blazes and looted what they could from numerous shops. By the time the fires were extinguished, large swathes of Patrick Street, along with City Hall and the Carnegie Library, were totally destroyed.

Following this attack, many Auxiliaries swaggered around Dublin with burnt corks attached to their Glengarries. Hamar Greenwood had to tell another 'Hamar' in the House of Commons, initially claiming, with enviable effrontery, that

Patrick Street after the burning of Cork city centre.
(Mercier Archive)

the city had been torched by Sinn Féin extremists, and then insisting that the fires spread from City Hall, a laughable idea considering it is on the other side of the river from Patrick Street, where the fire service reports clearly state that the first of the fires was started. The report of the military enquiry undertaken by General Strickland, the officer commanding the army in the Cork district, was not published because its effect 'would be disastrous to the government's whole policy in Ireland' – it clearly stated that the Auxiliaries started the fire and that there may have been RIC involvement as well. Over three million pounds was later paid out by the British government in compensation.

The horrors of the year were not yet over. On 15 December Canon Magner, parish priest of Dunmanway, and a young parishioner of his, Timothy Crowley, were shot dead by an Auxiliary officer on the side of the road, where they had stopped to help a local magistrate whose car had broken down. This happened a month after the body of Fr Michael Griffin, a priest from Barna in County Galway with known republican

Women, especially those in Cumann na mBan, played a crucial role in the war as fighters, couriers, intelligence agents, nurses, and organisers, as well as transporting weapons and ammunition around the country – they were fighting for real change for future generations and became experts in the use of propaganda. Their essential support was vital for the revolution to succeed.
(Mercier Archive)

sympathies, had been found riddled with bullets near his home the day after his arrest by crown forces.

As 1920 headed towards its murky close, two incidents took place that were characteristic of its violence. On 27 December the RIC carried out a raid on a big house, left vacant by its owners, at Bruff, County Limerick, where a dance was being held to raise funds for the East Limerick 3rd Battalion of the IRA. Five IRA men were shot and seventeen injured, while two Tans were killed in the assault. Then, on 29 December, an RIC patrol in Midleton, County Cork, was ambushed. Six men were shot, with three dying from their injuries. The town would be the scene of the first 'official reprisal' by soldiers on 1 January 1921, when seven houses were destroyed. Another year of apparently endless violence had begun.

COMING TO AN END

THE LAST six months of the war were its bloodiest: the number of police casualties from January to July was 241 – 62 more than for the whole of 1920. Of the civilians killed, a number were shot by the IRA as spies or, in some cases, for refusing to cooperate with the local brigade. An even greater number were deliberately shot by crown forces. Young men were particularly at risk from the Tans and Auxiliaries, whose lack of discipline and lawlessness eventually caused the latter's commander, Brigadier General Crozier, to resign on 19 February, after his attempts to punish members of the force who had looted Trim were overruled by General Tudor, the head of police. His rejection of the force as 'a drunken and insubordinate body of men' was no surprise to the people of Ireland and

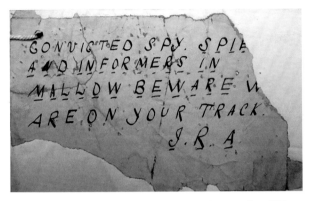

This label was found attached to the body of suspected spy William Alexander McPhearson, who was killed shortly before the Truce in Mallow, Cork. (Courtesy of Pádraig Óg Ó Ruairc)

was officially ignored by the British government. Yet it was another indictment of Lloyd George's conduct of Irish affairs and a further stimulus to moves to seek some cessation of the violence.

It was not only men who suffered. Female fatalities, while rarer, were not unknown. On 14 May 1921 DI Harry Biggs and the daughter of Sir Charles Barrington were killed on their way home from a fishing expedition at Newport, County Tipperary; two other women and an army officer escaped unharmed. The next day DI Cecil Blake and his wife were killed (she was shot five times) when their car was ambushed leaving a tennis match at Ballyturin House in Gort, County Galway. (The number of police fatalities for that May was the greatest for any month of the conflict.)

However, the incident that caused the greatest revulsion, amongst the British at least, was the kidnapping and shooting by the IRA of an elderly woman, Mrs Maria Lindsay, who had reported to the authorities that an ambush was being prepared near her home at Coachford, County Cork. She had also spoken to the local priest, who was meant to warn off the IRA, but when he attempted to do so, the local commander refused to take his information seriously. On foot of what Mrs Lindsay passed on, the IRA men were apprehended and five of them executed in Cork on 28 February; that same evening six off-duty soldiers were killed in Cork city. Mrs Lindsay, along with her chauffeur James Clarke, were kidnapped on 17 February and executed on 11 March.

IRA ambushes and individual assassinations continued, as did Tan and Auxiliary raids. On 7 March the serving Sinn Féin mayor of Limerick, George Clancy, a former mayor of Limerick

Michael O'Callaghan and prominent nationalist Joseph O'Donoghue were shot dead in their homes, almost a year after Tomás MacCurtain had been murdered in a similar fashion. There was a half-hearted attempt made to discipline the Tans and Auxiliaries, and more and more of the country was placed under martial law.

By this time the presence of de Valera, who had returned from America on 23 December

Auxiliaries searching civilians at Glanmire Road Station (now Kent Station) in Cork. (Mercier Archive)

1920, was beginning to have an effect. Although it may seem odd to the student of this period that such an important figure in the republican movement had found it necessary to spend nineteen months away from the war-torn country he was supposed to be leading, no one, least of all Collins, had cared either to try to prevent his going to America or to comment upon the length of his stay there. This would not be the last time that de Valera showed a capacity for making sure he could not be held responsible for the hard decisions that had to be made for the country's freedom.

However, de Valera's time in America had toughened him politically. On his arrival there he had found that he was no match for the Irish-American career politicians who, among other things, wished to wreck the League of Nations – President Woodrow Wilson's great hope for lasting peace. Wilson, heavily incapacitated in his last months of office by a stroke, turned out to be of no help when it came to securing recognition of Ireland's right to independence, and when, in November 1919, the Republican W. G.

W. G. Harding
(Courtesy of Library of Congress, LC-DIG-gg-bain-22827)

Harding (1865–1923) was elected president on an isolationist ticket without a single mention of Ireland during his campaign, it was clear that Ireland could expect no official support from America. Harding said, when asked to support Irish independence: 'I would not care to undertake to say to Great Britain what she must do, any more than I would permit her to tell us what we must do with the Philippines.'

On his return to Ireland, de Valera was deeply concerned about the effect that the military campaign was having upon the country and rather surprised at the prominent position that Collins had secured for himself. De Valera had little taste for guerrilla fighting; the lack of military uniform, though a considerable advantage for the IRA, meant that there could be no appeal to the Geneva Convention about things such as prisoners' rights, and Hamar Greenwood had made it clear that IRA internees in camps like Ballykinlar, near Dundrum in County Down, and in the various jails around the country would be held as prisoners of war without being given prisoner-of-war status, i.e. the right to humane treatment whilst incarcerated and with specific rules governing their release.

De Valera wanted to set the IRA's activities on a moral basis, regardless of the fact that the lack of such a foundation for their actions did not worry Collins or Brugha, let alone the various active brigades around the country. But as *príomh-aire* (prime minister) of Dáil Éireann, de Valera was in a position to insist that a formal state of war be declared against Britain. He urged a cutting-back in guerrilla activity: 'What we want is one good battle with about 500 men on each side.'

Such a 'good battle' took place, at his urging, on 25 May, when the Custom House in Dublin, where many local government records were stored, was burned by the IRA. However, British troops and Auxiliaries surrounded the building before the large raiding party could escape. Five

The Custom House burning.
(Mercier Archive)

*An Auxiliary searching the body of a man shot during
the burning of the Custom House.*
(Mercier Archive)

Volunteers were killed and at least eighty taken prisoner; the building, one of Dublin's architectural glories, burned for five days. The Auxiliaries suffered just five wounded. From Collins' point of view the action was a military disaster and did nothing to improve the increasingly strained relations between him and de Valera. Yet coming when it did, at a time when Lloyd George's government could no longer bear the increasing disintegration of its reputation abroad, especially in America, it proved to be a political success.

This, added to the erosion of support for British rule even amongst loyalists in the southern counties of Ireland, due to the indiscriminate reprisals that were still being carried out by British forces, meant that something had to give.

By this stage Lloyd George's position within the government coalition was not strong. The prime minister's own Liberal Party was now in a minority and dependent on the grace and favour of the Conservatives, who were still strongly opposed to any kind of settlement with the Irish republicans. Lloyd George also had to face down his generals, who were claiming that they could finish the war in Britain's favour if he removed the political constraints under which they operated. Surprisingly, however, the move towards a more peaceful resolution of the Irish situation was supported by Churchill, whose political antennae were even more sensitive than de Valera's, and who came out strongly in favour of a truce.

The increasing casualty rate sustained by the police and army in Ireland throughout 1921, which made it clear that they were no closer to a military victory, and the growing international pressure to find a peaceful solution eventually led to the start of negotiations for a truce. Further pressure was added when the May 1921 elections in the twenty-six counties saw landslide victories for republican candidates across the board.

The main stumbling block to previous attempts at a truce was the British demand that the IRA surrender its arms before any talks commenced. As early as November 1920 the archbishop of Perth, P. J. Clune, whose nephew Conor was one of those killed on Bloody Sunday, had been in serious talks with the British regarding a truce, but these had broken down over the British refusal to waive this demand. Another stumbling block had been the British refusal to allow Collins to take part in any negotiations for a peace deal.

One of the main negotiators in this earlier attempt had been Alfred 'Andy' Cope, the assistant under-secretary for Ireland in Dublin Castle. He would also be a major player in the renewed attempts and was one of the tireless heroes of the process. The arrest in June of de Valera, who was now president of the second Dáil – which had 124 Sinn Féin members, all elected unopposed – was an embarrassment that Cope had to deal with. De Valera, whose cooperation was essential if any deal were to be achieved, was released a day later.

The need for an agreed solution was now urgent. The Government of Ireland Act had come into force in May 1921 and the new Northern Irish parliament was formally opened by King George V on 22 June. During the ceremony the

Sir James Craig (left), the first prime minister of Northern Ireland, at the opening of the Northern Ireland Parliament at Stormont, Belfast, on 22 June 1921. (Courtesy of Kilmainham Gaol Museum, 19PC-1B51-04)

king gave a speech, written for him by Lloyd George, with a significant contribution by Jan Smuts, the famous Boer War general and peace-maker, urging 'all Irishmen to pause, to stretch out the hand of forbearance and conciliation, to forgive and forget, and to join in making for the land which they love a new era of peace, content-ment and good will'.

The British government was now facing a deadline of mid-July, by which time either order was to be restored in southern Ireland or the twenty-six counties would revert to the position of a crown colony. This would entail draconian measures being imposed on Ireland, including membership of the Dáil and the IRA being considered treasonous and punishable by death; it was reckoned that it would require 100,000 troops to maintain order. With no let-up in IRA activity and deafening criticism even from the British newspapers, the pressure to find a solution became overwhelming.

The men of the IRA, especially its members in the south and west, who were by now veteran warriors, were not likely to be impressed by the sentiments expressed by King George in such a place on the occasion of the formal partitioning of the country. The IRA was, however, in need of respite: Collins reckoned that if the Truce had not come into effect, resistance could not have continued for more than a few weeks.

Unaware of this, Lloyd George removed all his previous conditions about personnel and the laying down of arms, and a truce was concluded in the Mansion House between General Macready and his aide Colonel Brind on the British side, and Éamonn Duggan and Robert Barton for the Irish. It came into effect at noon on 11 July. The conditions included a cessation of attacks on crown forces and civilians, the avoidance of provocative displays of force, and no reinforcement of men or arms by either side; these provisions were to apply to the areas still under martial law, as well as the rest of the country.

The violence continued right up to the noon deadline, with three RIC men being killed or fatally wounded in incidents across the country on that morning. Constable Alexander Clarke, was the last victim; he was shot in Skibbereen,

The scene outside Dublin Castle a few moments after the Truce came into effect at noon on 11 July 1921. Members of the public and Auxiliaries gathered, expecting a formal announcement, but none was made. (Mercier Archive)

County Cork as he was walking to his lodgings in Townsend Street.

The Truce was fragile, but it held. It took some time for the realisation that the country was again at peace to sink in. One slightly cynical, if not unexpected, result of the end of hostilities was the increase in numbers joining the IRA – the 'Trucileers' as an anonymous Irish wit was to call them. Those who had fought in constant danger of their lives on both sides were glad of the at least temporary lull, but Collins and the other leaders understood the risk the IRA was taking: 'like rabbits coming out of their holes'. Moreover, ominous cracks were beginning to appear in the smooth façade of IRA unity, cracks which became the rift that led to civil war.

Yet for the time being, throughout the twenty-six counties there was a light-headed sense that maybe now things would get better. The war had generated plenty of new Irish heroes – Tom Barry, Liam Deasy, Seán Treacy, Dan Breen, Ernie O'Malley, Oscar Traynor, Liam Lynch and Seán MacEoin, among others. But not all the Volunteers were heroes, just as not all their adversaries were villains. While some of the British were – and still are – granted a grudging respect, someone who is still reviled to this day is Major Arthur Percival of the Essex Regiment, who liked to ride about south Cork in an open car with a loaded gun in his hands, looking for targets. He was undoubtedly responsible for the torture of prisoners and was lucky to escape with his life.

During the Civil War both sides accused the other of being Trucileers or Trucers – supposed patriots who had only joined the IRA after the War of Independence was over.
(Mercier Archive)

He lived to face the humiliation, as Lieutenant General Percival, of surrendering his army to a much smaller Japanese force in Singapore on 15 February 1942 during the Second World War, following 'the greatest military defeat in the history of the British Empire'.

When the terms of the Truce were published, political and sectarian tensions in the north increased and a week of rioting in Belfast followed an IRA attack on an RIC patrol there.

Members of the RIC and Special Constabulary joined forces with loyalist mobs over the Twelfth holiday and the violence resulted in the deaths of sixteen Catholics and seven Protestants, and the destruction of over 200 Catholic homes. There was nothing new in anti-Catholic pogroms, but the appalled minority nationalist population in the north was beginning to understand what the Government of Ireland Act would mean for them.

The IRA and their late adversaries had other things on their minds, with the negotiations in London for a treaty that would lead to a permanent peace. But it is difficult, even at this distance, to understand why they allowed the promise of a boundary commission to blind their eyes to the reality of the future of a divided island.

Collins, de Valera and their comrades were entitled to their moment of triumph, but they were yet to learn the truth of the words of David Neligan, one of Collins' Castle moles, in his book *The Spy in the Castle*: 'Revolution devours her own children'.

British troops lower the Union flag during the handover of Victoria Barracks in Cork city in early 1922 as part of the military evacuation of the British after the signing of the Anglo-Irish Treaty. (Mercier Archive)

BIOGRAPHICAL INDEX

Thomas Ashe (1885–1917) was born in Lispole, County Kerry and trained as a teacher, becoming the principal of Lusk National School in north County Dublin. He was active in the Gaelic League and was commander of the Fingal Battalion of Volunteers. He featured in the greatest military success of the Rising, the ambush of an RIC detachment at Ashbourne on the Friday of Easter Week. He was sentenced to life imprisonment but released in 1917. Rearrested, he organised a hunger strike in Mountjoy for political status for Sinn Féin prisoners and died as a result of injury from force-feeding.

Herbert Henry Asquith (1852–1928) was Liberal prime minister of the UK from 1908 to 1916, when he was replaced by David Lloyd George. The Rising found him at his weakest politically and he allowed General Maxwell too much power in its aftermath.

Kevin Barry (1902–20) was born in Dublin and joined the Irish Volunteers in 1917 while still at Belvedere School. On 20 September 1920, while a medical student at UCD, he took part in an ambush in which a young soldier was killed. Found hiding under a cart in possession of a revolver, Barry was sentenced to be hanged. His execution, on 1 November, prompted widespread criticism.

Tom Barry (1897–1980) was born in Rosscarbery, County Cork, the son of a policeman who had bought a pub on his retirement. He joined the British Army in 1915 and served in the Mesopotamia Expeditionary Force. After the war he enrolled in a business college in Cork but was approached by Volunteers as a man of known military experience. He led the highly disciplined West Cork flying column – a concept in guerrilla warfare he largely developed. In November 1920 he led the Kilmichael ambush, in which the Auxiliaries suffered their most serious defeat, and in March 1921 at Crossbarry successfully engaged a superior force from the Essex Regiment. He took the anti-Treaty side in the Civil War and continued as a member of the IRA until 1938, when he resigned because he disagreed with the organisation's bombing campaign in Britain. He subsequently published *Guerilla Days in Ireland* (1949), an account of his activities during the War of Independence.

Robert Barton (1881–1975), a cousin of Erskine Childers, was born in County Wicklow and educated at Rugby and Oxford. He resigned from the British Army in 1916 and joined the IRA. Minister for agriculture in the first Dáil, he helped negotiate the terms of the Truce. He was one of the signatories of the Treaty, recommending it as 'the lesser of two outrages', but remained a supporter of de Valera. He was chairman of the Agricultural Credit Corporation (1934–54) and later of Bord na Móna.

Dan Breen (1894–1969) was a farmer's son, born in Donohill, County Tipperary. He was part of the attack at Soloheadbeg, widely accepted as the first action of the War of Independence. He was also active in Dublin, making an attempt on the life of the lord lieutenant, among other things. He fought on the anti-Treaty side in Tipperary during the Civil War until he was captured on 17 April 1923. He was the first opponent of the Treaty to actually sit in the Dáil, taking his seat in January 1927. He served as Fianna Fáil TD for Tipperary South from 1932 to 1965. His autobiography, *My Fight for Irish Freedom* (first published in 1924), contains an account of his guerrilla years.

Eamon 'Ned' Broy (1887–1972) was born in County Kildare and worked as a clerk in the DMP from 1911 with the rank of detective sergeant. He became one of Collins' most successful agents in Dublin Castle, supplying him with early information about police intentions. He was arrested in February 1921 and jailed for six months. After the Treaty he was made an adjutant in the National Army and then promoted to colonel. He succeeded Eoin O'Duffy as commissioner of An Garda Síochána and formed an Auxiliary Special Branch which became known as 'Broy's Harriers'. He was always interested in athletics and became president of the Irish Olympic Council in 1935.

Cathal Brugha (1874–1922) was born Charles Burgess in Dublin. He joined the Gaelic League in 1899 and the Volunteers in 1913. He was second-in-command to Éamonn Ceannt in the South Dublin Union during Easter Week and was so badly wounded on the Thursday that he was permanently lame. He was a strong opponent of the Treaty and was shot in Thomas' Lane, Dublin at the start of the Civil War.

Erskine Childers (1870–1922) was born in London but was reared in Wicklow. He was educated at Haileybury and Cambridge and saw service in the Boer War. An expert mariner (his novel *The Riddle of the Sands*, postulating a German invasion of Britain, was a bestseller in 1903 and has never been out of print since), he brought a shipment of arms for the Irish Volunteers into Howth in July 1914. He served in the Royal Navy Air Service during the Great War and succeeded Desmond FitzGerald as director of publicity for the Volunteers during the War of Independence, editing the propagandist and extremely successful *Irish Bulletin*. Though a member of the Treaty delegation, he rejected the Treaty's terms. He was captured on 10 November 1922 and executed by firing squad by government forces on 24 November for being in possession of a revolver, a gift from his friend Michael Collins.

Winston Churchill (1874–1965) was the eldest son of Lord Randolph Churchill and born in Blenheim Palace, the home of his relation, the Duke of Marlborough. While secretary of state for war and air in Lloyd George's coalition (1918–21), he advocated the criminalisation of IRA activities, refusing to regard it as a legitimate army at war, but he was an active member of the Treaty negotiations and supported the Free State. After many years as a political maverick, he became prime minister on the fall of Neville Chamberlain and was one of the significant leaders in the Second World War. He refused all royal honours except the exclusive Order of Merit and, later, a knighthood. He won the Nobel Prize for Literature in 1953.

Michael Collins (1890–1922) was born in Clonakilty, County Cork, and served as a postal clerk in the British civil service in London. He joined the IRB in 1915 and was one of the survivors of Easter Week. By the time he was released from Frongoch internment camp in December 1916 he was an important leader in the movement and played a major role in its reorganisation. During the War of Independence he was a brilliant and ruthless head of military intelligence. He was a reluctant member of the Treaty delegation but regarded the terms as the best that were possible in the circumstances. Though he had little experience of actual guerrilla fighting, he was commander-in-chief of the Free State forces at the start of the Civil War. He was killed in an ambush in Béal na mBláth, not far from his birthplace, on 22 August 1922.

Alfred Cope (1877–1954), known popularly as 'Andy', was a career politician and served as assistant under-secretary to Sir Hamar Green-wood during the War of Independence. He was one of the most active and successful parties in bringing about the Truce and he assisted General Macready in supervising the withdrawal of British troops from Ireland. He was knighted in 1922.

Frank Percy Crozier (1879–1937) was a career soldier of Ulster extraction who fought in both the Boer War and the Great War, training the UVF in the interval. He rose to the rank of brigadier and was active in the Lithuanian Army against the Bolsheviks. He assumed command of the Auxiliary Division but resigned in February 1921 when his attempts to discipline the force were frustrated by General Tudor. He wrote a number of books of memoir, including *Ireland for Ever* (1932), which was remarkably pro-nationalist.

Éamon de Valera (1882–1975) was born in New York but was brought up in County Limerick from the age of two. He became a lecturer in mathematics and joined the Gaelic League in 1908 and the Volunteers in 1913. Commander at Boland's Mills during Easter Week, he was the only 1916 leader to survive a sentence of execution. He was president of the first Dáil

Éireann and the first leader to meet Lloyd George after the Truce which ended the War of Independence in 1921. He refused to lead the Treaty delegation and rejected the terms agreed by Collins and Griffith, but was largely inactive during the Civil War. His greatest post-war achievement was the politicisation of the republican movement by the founding of the Fianna Fáil party, which he led as taoiseach in four governments. He also served two terms as president of Ireland (1959–73).

Liam Deasy (1898–1974) was born near Bandon, County Cork, and was adjutant of the West Cork Brigade of the IRA during the Anglo-Irish War. He rejected the Treaty and though he fought in the Civil War, he was greatly distressed by its effects. He believed that the surrender of the Four Courts in July 1922 should have been the end rather than the beginning of hostilities. He was captured by government forces in January 1923 and, convinced that the time had come to end the fighting, signed a document worded for him by his captors that he was in favour of unconditional surrender. After the war he took no further part in public life but served throughout the Emergency in the Irish Army. He published an account of the brigade's activities, *Towards Ireland Free*, and a book on the Civil War, *Brother against Brother*.

John Devoy (1842–1928) was born in Kill, County Kildare, and served in both the French Foreign Legion and the British Army, where he became a Fenian spy. He helped in the rescue of the Fenian 'chief' James Stephens from Richmond Jail in 1865 and, given fifteen years' imprisonment for organising Fenian 'cells', was amnestied having served five years, on condition that he leave the United Kingdom. He led Clan na Gael in America and supported all anti-British movements in Ireland thereafter, including the Land War and the Rising. He died in Atlantic City.

Éamonn Duggan (1874–1936) was born in County Meath and qualified as a solicitor in 1914. He was arrested after the Easter Rising and later became director of IRA intelligence. He was elected to the first Dáil in 1918, imprisoned in 1920 and subsequently released to take part in the Mansion House talks that led to the Truce. He was one of the signatories of the Treaty and held several posts in W. T. Cosgrave's government, retiring in 1933 to become a senator.

John Denton French, First Earl of Ypres (1852–1925) was born in Kent into a family with property in County Roscommon. He joined the Royal Navy when he was fourteen but later transferred to the army. After a successful career as a cavalry officer in the Sudan and during the Boer War, he became chief of the imperial staff in 1912. Forced to resign because of his support for the anti-Home Rule officers in the Curragh, he was recalled to lead the British Expeditionary Force in 1914 when the Great War began. General Douglas Haig replaced him in 1915 due to his erratic performance. He was made lord lieutenant of Ireland in 1918, resigning in 1921 with a gratuity of £50,000 after a period of office in which he demonstrated a lack of under-standing of the Irish situation. During this time many attempts were made on his life, the most dangerous one involving the Squad, with Dan Breen and Seán Treacy, on 19 December 1919.

Frank Gallagher (1893–1962) was born in Cork and was deputy to Erskine Childers on the staff of the Volunteer news-sheet the *Irish Bulletin*, which presented the activities of the IRA in the best possible light and was extremely influential in winning international support for the Irish cause. He was the first editor of *The Irish Press* (1931–95) and later worked for Radio Éireann and the National Library.

David Lloyd George (1863–1945) was born in Manchester but was brought up in Caernarvonshire in Wales. He had a brilliant career as a Liberal reformer, associated with old-age pensions, National Insurance and the taming of the House of Lords. He was minister of munitions, secretary of state for war and, having ousted Asquith, prime minister from 1916, proving a highly efficient war leader. Sympathetic to the Ulster unionists, as early as 1916 he decided to exclude them from the rule of an Irish parliament according to their wishes. Slow to give the War of Independence the political attention it deserved, he tried an ineffectual mixture of conciliation and coercion until forced to seek an end to the fighting through the Truce. It was his threat of 'war within three days' that persuaded Griffith and Collins to accept the Treaty terms. A scandal over selling knighthoods and peerages, followed by opposition to British foreign policy in Turkey forced his resignation as prime minister in 1922.

Hamar Greenwood (1870–1948) was born in Canada and came to live in England in 1895. He was called to the bar in 1906 and was elected as a Liberal MP in the same year. He served in France in the Great War (1914–16) and was made a baronet in 1915. He was appointed chief secretary for Ireland on 12 April 1920 and, though it caused him some private embarrassment, he publicly defended the excesses of the Tans and Auxiliaries. He took little part in the pre-Truce talks, though he was present during the Treaty negotiations. He resigned in October 1922, and later followed Churchill's lead and joined the Conservative Party. He became a viscount in 1937.

Arthur Griffith (1871–1922) was born in Dublin and became a journalist. He was a member of the Gaelic League and the IRB, and founded Sinn Féin, which advocated Irish self-sufficiency and passive resistance as the best means of ending British governance of Ireland. He opposed the Home Rule Bill of 1914 and was arrested after the Easter Rising, although he had not been a participant. Released by the general amnesty, he was re-arrested at the time of the 'German Plot' in 1918. He was elected MP for East Cavan while still in prison and was acting president of the Dáil while de Valera was in America (1919–20). He was arrested in November 1920 but was released shortly before the Truce in July 1921. He led the Treaty delegation in December of that year and was its first signatory. Elected president of the Dáil when de Valera resigned in January 1922, he died of a cerebral haemorrhage on 12 August that year, worn out by the strain of the negotiations and the Civil War caused by the rejection by some of the Treaty terms.

Andrew Bonar Law (1858–1923) was born in Canada but lived in Scotland from age twelve. He worked as an iron merchant in Glasgow, serving as an MP from 1910. He replaced Arthur Balfour as the Conservative Party's leader in the House of Commons. He actively supported Ulster's resistance to Home Rule and left Lloyd George with little room to manoeuvre during the Treaty negotiations. He replaced him as prime minister in 1923, but resigned due to illness in May of that year.

Liam Lynch (1893–1923) was born in County Limerick. At seventeen he started an apprenticeship in a hardware business in Mitchelstown, County Cork and in 1919 he organised the Cork Volunteers. He was an able brigade commander during the War of Independence. He opposed the Treaty but was anxious to avoid further conflict. However, after the Civil War broke out, he became the most implacable of the anti-Treaty commanders. He led the Southern Division of the anti-Treatyites and hoped to hold a

'Munster Republic' against Free State forces. He was mortally wounded in the Knockmealdown mountains on 10 April 1923.

Tomás MacCurtain (1884–1920) was born in County Cork and was a member of the Gaelic League and commander of the Cork Volunteers. With Terence MacSwiney, he organised the local Volunteers in preparation for the Easter Rising, although the general confusion at the start of Easter Week meant that little action occurred in Cork. After his release from internment, he remained active in the movement and also became the first Sinn Féin lord mayor of Cork. He was assassinated at his home by a gang of masked raiders.

Seán MacEoin (1893–1973), known as the 'Blacksmith of Ballinalee' (in County Longford), led a flying column there during the War of Independence. He supported the Treaty and became chief of staff of the Free State army. He resigned in 1929 to become a full-time TD (he had also served in the Dáil from 1921–23) and served as Fine Gael minister in both the inter-party governments. He stood unsuccessfully for the presidency in 1945 and 1959.

Cecil Frederick Nevil Macready (1862–1945) was born in Cheltenham, the son of the

Shakespearean actor William Macready (1793–1873), himself of Irish extraction, who sired him at age sixty-nine. In 1881 he joined the Gordon Highlanders and was general officer commanding Belfast before becoming adjutant general in the British Expeditionary Force. Promoted to brigadier in 1918, he served as commissioner of the London Metropolitan Police (1918–20) before being persuaded to accept the post of general officer commanding in Ireland by his old commander, Lord French. Though disclaiming any trace of Irishness, his code of military conduct made him publicly decry the behaviour of the Black and Tans and the Auxies. He was active in seeking the basis for a truce, was present at discussions with de Valera, Griffith and Jan Smuts in July 1921 and worked out the terms of the Truce with Robert Barton and Éamonn Duggan. He oversaw the withdrawal of British forces in January 1922 and retired from the army in 1923.

Terence MacSwiney (1879–1920) was born in Cork and, with Tomás MacCurtain, organised the Volunteers in anticipation of the Easter Rising. He succeeded MacCurtain as lord mayor of Cork after the latter's murder in March 1920. Arrested under the Defence of the Realm Act in August 1920, he went on hunger strike in Brixton. He died on 25 October after seventy-four days on hunger strike, during which all appeals for his release went unheeded, but the publicity surrounding his protracted death was very damaging to Britain's reputation in Europe, Australia and America.

General Sir John Maxwell (1859–1929) arrived in Dublin as general officer commanding the military on 28 April 1916. He insisted upon a complete and urgent defeat of the Volunteers. Instigating martial law, he was the only authority in Ireland for the next critical month and the policy of paced executions and massive arrests was his. He retired from the army in 1922.

Richard Mulcahy (1886–1971) was born in Waterford and worked as a post office clerk. He was involved in the ambush at Ashbourne during Easter Week and after the general amnesty became a senior figure in the IRA. He supported the Treaty and as commander-in-chief after Collins' death was vigorous in his activity against the anti-Treatyites. He was one of the founders of the Fine Gael party in 1933 and, precluded because of his Civil War reputation from the post of taoiseach in the coalition governments of the 1940s and 1950s, served as minister for education under John A. Costello.

Ernie O'Malley (1898–1957) was born in Castlebar and was a medical student in UCD when he fought in Easter Week. He was active during the War of Independence and, opposing the Treaty, was appointed a member of the IRA Army Council in October 1922. He was badly wounded and captured by government forces in November 1922; having recovered from his wounds he went on a hunger strike which lasted for forty-one days in Mountjoy. His death sentence was commuted when the surgeons said he would never walk again. He was elected abstentionist TD for North Dublin in 1923 and released in July 1924. Having recovered the use of his limbs, he travelled widely and was one of the chief fundraisers for *The Irish Press*. His accounts of his experiences in the War of Independence – *On Another Man's Wound* (1936) – and the Civil War – *The Singing Flame* (1978) – are regarded as the finest literary record of the two conflicts.

John Redmond (1856–1918) was born in County Wexford. He became chairman of the IPP in 1900, having healed the rift caused by the fall of Charles Stewart Parnell. Holding the balance of power in the Commons in 1910, he was able to get Asquith to introduce a Home Rule bill. On the outbreak of the First World War, he encouraged recruitment to the British Army, and briefly supported Asquith's decision to make an example of the ringleaders of the Rising. His party was soundly defeated in the 1918 general election and he died in March of that year.

Jan Christian Smuts (1870–1950) was born in the Cape Colony and led the guerrilla forces in the Boer War (1899–1902). He was a key figure in the peace negotiations and in the setting up of the Union of South Africa in 1910. He served in the British war cabinets in both world wars but was unable to overcome the rise of Afrikaans nationalism. The defeat of his pro-Commonwealth United Party by the National Party in 1948 led to the setting up of the union as a republic outside the commonwealth. He was one of the prime movers in arranging the truce that ended the Irish War of Independence in 1921 and is credited as the main architect of the speech of George V at the opening of the Northern Ireland parliament on 22 June 1921 that helped persuade the British to make every effort to secure a cessation of the fighting.

Austin Stack (1879–1929) was born near Tralee, County Kerry, and was arrested for his involvement in the attempted landing of arms by Sir Roger Casement (1864–1916) at Banna Strand in April 1916. He was minister for home affairs in the first Dáil, rejected the terms of the Treaty and was active in the Civil War until his capture in April 1923. During his imprisonment in Kilmainham he led a hunger strike for forty-one days, an ordeal from which his health never recovered.

Oscar Traynor (1886–1963) was born in Dublin and trained as a wood-carver and compositor. He took part in the 1916 Rising and was interned at Frongoch. Commander of the Dublin Brigade of the IRA, he led the attack on the Custom House on 25 May 1921. He opposed the Treaty and continued to organise military activity in Wicklow after the anti-Treatyites lost the battle for Dublin. He served in most Fianna Fáil governments until his resignation because of ill-health in 1961. A noted footballer, he played for Belfast Celtic when he was a young man and was president of the FAI from 1948 until his death.

Seán Treacy (1895–1920) was a leading Gaelic League organiser in South Tipperary and a member of the Irish Volunteers. With Dan Breen he was part of the Soloheadbeg ambush that began the War of Independence. He and Breen were involved in an attempt to assassinate the viceroy, Lord French, in Dublin in December 1919. He was killed in a gun battle in Talbot Street, Dublin, on 14 October 1920.

Henry Hugh Tudor (1871–1965) was born in Devon and was wounded in action in both the Boer War and the First World War. Appointed chief of the Irish police services in 1920, holding his military rank of major general, he oversaw the reinforcement of the RIC with the Black and Tans and the Auxiliary Division. He was constant in his defence of the new recruits but admitted that there was much drunkenness and indiscipline among them, blaming it on the conditions under which they had to operate. He initiated the use of the aeroplane as a counter-terrorist weapon. Subsequently, he was general officer commanding and inspector of police and prisons in Palestine.

SELECT BIBLIOGRAPHY

Abbott, R., *Police Casualties in Ireland 1919–1922* (revised edition, Cork, 2019)

Barry, T., *Guerilla Days in Ireland* (Cork, 1958)

Beckett, J. C., *The Making of Modern Ireland, 1603–1923* (London, 1966)

Breen, D., *My Fight for Irish Freedom* (revised edition, Dublin, 1964)

Coffey, T. M., *Agony at Easter: The 1916 Irish Uprising* (London, 1970)

Collins, M., *The Path to Freedom: Articles and Speeches of Michael Collins* (Cork, 2018)

Coogan, T. P., *Michael Collins* (London, 1990)

Deasy, L., *Towards Ireland Free* (Cork, 1973)

— *Brother against Brother* (Cork, 1994)

Department of External Affairs, *Cuimhneachán 1916–1966* (Dublin, 1966)

Doherty, G. and Keogh, D. (eds), *Michael Collins and the Making of the Irish State* (Dublin, 1998)

Doherty, J. E. and Hickey, D. J., *A Chronology of Irish History Since 1500* (Dublin, 1989)

Dwyer, T. Ryle, *Michael Collins: The Man Who Won the War* (Cork, 1990)

— *De Valera: The Man and the Myths* (Dublin, 1991)

— *The Squad and the Intelligence Operations of Michael Collins* (Cork, 2005)

Fanning, R., *Independent Ireland* (Dublin, 1983)

Foster, R. F., *Modern Ireland 1600–1972* (London, 1988)

— (ed.), *The Oxford History of Ireland* (Oxford, 1989)

Gillis, Liz, *Revolution in Dublin: A Photographic History 1913–1923* (Cork, 2013)

— *Women of the Irish Revolution 1913-1923: A Photographic History* (Cork, 2014)

— *The Hales Brothers and the Irish Revolution* (Cork, 2016)

Griffith, K. and O'Grady, T. (eds), *Curious Journey: An Oral History of Ireland's Unfinished Revolution* (Cork, 1998)

Hart, P., *The IRA and Its Enemies* (Oxford, 1998)

Horgan, T., *Fighting for the Cause: Kerry's Republican Fighters* (Cork, 2018)

Keane, B., *Cork's Revolutionary Dead 1916–1923* (Cork, 2017)

Kee, R., *The Green Flag* (London, 1970)

Kiberd, D., *Inventing Ireland: The Literature of the Modern Nation* (London, 1995)

Lee, J. J., *Ireland 1912–1985* (Cambridge, 1989)

Lenihan, M., *Cork Burning* (Cork, 2018)

Lyons, F. S. L., *Ireland Since The Famine* (London, 1971)

Mac Lochlainn, P. F., *Last Words: Letters and Statements of the Leaders Executed after the Rising at Easter 1916* (Dublin, 1971)

Macardle, D., *The Irish Republic* (revised edition, Dublin 1968)

Matthews, A., *Renegades: Irish Republican Women 1900–1922* (Cork, 2010)

McHugh, R. (ed.), *Dublin 1916* (London, 1966)

Neligan, D., *The Spy in the Castle* (London, 1968)

O'Connor, F., *The Big Fellow: Michael Collins and the Irish Revolution* (Cork, 2018)

Ó Duibhir, L., *Prisoners of War: Ballykinlar Internment Camp 1920–1921* (Cork, 2013)

Ó Gadhra, N., *Civil War in Connacht 1922–1923* (Cork, 1999)

O'Malley, E., *On Another Man's Wound* (Dublin, 1936)

— *The Singing Flame* (Dublin, 1978)

— *The Men Will Talk to Me: Clare Interviews,* ed. P. Óg Ó Ruairc (Cork, 2016)

Ó Ruairc, P. Óg, *Blood on the Banner: The Republican Struggle in Clare* (Cork, 2009)

— *Revolution: A Photographic History of Revolutionary Ireland 1913–1923* (Cork, 2014)

— *Truce: Murder, Myth and the Last Days of the Irish War of Independence* (Cork, 2016)

Ó Súilleabháin, M., *Where Mountainy Men Have Sown: War and Peace in Rebel Cork in the Turbulent Years 1916–21* (Cork, 2013)

Ryan, D., *The Rising* (Dublin, 1949)

Ryan, M., *Tom Barry: IRA Freedom Fighter* (Cork, 2011)

— *Liam Lynch, The Real Chief* (Cork, 2012)

Welch, R. (ed.), *The Oxford Companion to Irish Literature* (Oxford, 1996)

INDEX